NAME	
CONTACT NUMBER	
EMAIL	
COMPANY	
FAX NUMBER	
WEBSITE	

EMERGENCY DETAILS

NAME:	NAME:
CONTACT NUMBER:	CONTACT NUMBER:

www.signatureplannerjournals.com
www.signatureplannerjournals.co.uk

DATE	/	/	**DAY**	M	T	W	T	F	S	Su

FOREMAN	
PROJECT/ JOB	

CONTRACT No.	

WEATHER (Hot, Rain, Windy etc.)	**SAFETY MEETING**

	SAFETY MEETING
YES	NO	Subject:

CONCERNS/ ACTIONS:

TEMPERATURE	
AM	**PM**

GROUND CONDITIONS
(Wet, Dry, Frozen, Damp)

VISITORS (Name, Company, Reason)

SCHEDULE	
Completion Date	
Days Ahead	
Days Behind	

PROBLEMS/ DELAYS

SAFETY ISSUES

ACCIDENTS/ INCIDENTS (Who, Where, When, Contact)

SUMMARY OF WORK PERFORMED TODAY

SIGNATURE		TITLE

EMPLOYEE	Craft	Contracted Hrs.	Overtime	Subcontractors	Craft	Hours Worked

EQUIPMENT ON SITE	No. Units	Working	
		Yes	No

MATERIALS DELIVERED	No. Units	Materials Rented	From & Rate

NOTES

DATE	/	/	**DAY**	M	T	W	T	F	S	Su

FOREMAN	
PROJECT/ JOB		CONTRACT No.	

WEATHER (Hot, Rain, Windy etc.)	**SAFETY MEETING**		
	YES	NO	Subject:
	CONCERNS/ ACTIONS:		

TEMPERATURE	
AM	**PM**

GROUND CONDITIONS (Wet, Dry, Frozen, Damp)

VISITORS (Name, Company, Reason)

SCHEDULE	
Completion Date	
Days Ahead	
Days Behind	

PROBLEMS/ DELAYS

SAFETY ISSUES

ACCIDENTS/ INCIDENTS (Who, Where, When, Contact)

SUMMARY OF WORK PERFORMED TODAY

SIGNATURE	TITLE

EMPLOYEE	Craft	Contracted Hrs.	Overtime		Subcontractors	Craft	Hours Worked

EQUIPMENT ON SITE	No. Units	Working	
		Yes	No

MATERIALS DELIVERED	No. Units	Materials Rented	From & Rate

NOTES

DATE	/	/	**DAY**	M	T	W	T	F	S	Su
FOREMAN										
PROJECT/ JOB			CONTRACT No.							

WEATHER (Hot, Rain, Windy etc.)		SAFETY MEETING			
		YES	NO	Subject:	
		CONCERNS/ ACTIONS:			

TEMPERATURE

AM	PM

GROUND CONDITIONS
(Wet, Dry, Frozen, Damp)

VISITORS (Name, Company, Reason)

SCHEDULE

Completion Date	
Days Ahead	
Days Behind	

PROBLEMS/ DELAYS

SAFETY ISSUES

ACCIDENTS/ INCIDENTS (Who, Where, When, Contact)

SUMMARY OF WORK PERFORMED TODAY

SIGNATURE	TITLE

EMPLOYEE	Craft	Contracted Hrs.	Overtime	Subcontractors	Craft	Hours Worked

EQUIPMENT ON SITE	No. Units	Working	
		Yes	No

MATERIALS DELIVERED	No. Units	Materials Rented	From & Rate

NOTES

DATE	/	/	**DAY**	M	T	W	T	F	S	Su

FOREMAN	

PROJECT/ JOB		CONTRACT No.	

WEATHER (Hot, Rain, Windy etc.)	**SAFETY MEETING**		

	YES	NO	Subject:

CONCERNS/ ACTIONS:

TEMPERATURE

AM	PM

GROUND CONDITIONS
(Wet, Dry, Frozen, Damp)

VISITORS (Name, Company, Reason)

SCHEDULE

Completion Date	
Days Ahead	
Days Behind	

PROBLEMS/ DELAYS

SAFETY ISSUES

ACCIDENTS/ INCIDENTS (Who, Where, When, Contact)

SUMMARY OF WORK PERFORMED TODAY

SIGNATURE		TITLE

EMPLOYEE	Craft	Contracted Hrs.	Overtime		Subcontractors	Craft	Hours Worked

EQUIPMENT ON SITE	No. Units	Working	
		Yes	No

MATERIALS DELIVERED	No. Units	Materials Rented	From & Rate

NOTES

DATE	/	/	**DAY**	M	T	W	T	F	S	Su

FOREMAN	

PROJECT/ JOB		CONTRACT No.	

WEATHER (Hot, Rain, Windy etc.)	**SAFETY MEETING**		

	YES	NO	Subject:

CONCERNS/ ACTIONS:

TEMPERATURE	
AM	**PM**

GROUND CONDITIONS (Wet, Dry, Frozen, Damp)

VISITORS (Name, Company, Reason)

SCHEDULE		**PROBLEMS/ DELAYS**
Completion Date		
Days Ahead		
Days Behind		

SAFETY ISSUES	ACCIDENTS/ INCIDENTS (Who, Where, When, Contact)

SUMMARY OF WORK PERFORMED TODAY

SIGNATURE		TITLE

EMPLOYEE	Craft	Contracted Hrs.	Overtime	Subcontractors	Craft	Hours Worked

EQUIPMENT ON SITE	No. Units	Working	
		Yes	No

MATERIALS DELIVERED	No. Units	Materials Rented	From & Rate

NOTES

DATE	/	/	**DAY**	M	T	W	T	F	S	Su
FOREMAN										

PROJECT/ JOB		**CONTRACT No.**	

WEATHER (Hot, Rain, Windy etc.)	**SAFETY MEETING**		
	YES	NO	Subject:
	CONCERNS/ ACTIONS:		

TEMPERATURE	
AM	**PM**

GROUND CONDITIONS
(Wet, Dry, Frozen, Damp)

VISITORS (Name, Company, Reason)

SCHEDULE	
Completion Date	
Days Ahead	
Days Behind	

PROBLEMS/ DELAYS

SAFETY ISSUES

ACCIDENTS/ INCIDENTS (Who, Where, When, Contact)

SUMMARY OF WORK PERFORMED TODAY

SIGNATURE	TITLE

EMPLOYEE	Craft	Contracted Hrs.	Overtime		Subcontractors	Craft	Hours Worked

EQUIPMENT ON SITE	No. Units	Working	
		Yes	No

MATERIALS DELIVERED	No. Units	Materials Rented	From & Rate

NOTES

DATE	/ /	**DAY**	M	T	W	T	F	S	Su

FOREMAN	
PROJECT/ JOB		CONTRACT No.	

WEATHER (Hot, Rain, Windy etc.)	**SAFETY MEETING**

		YES	**NO**	Subject:

CONCERNS/ ACTIONS:

TEMPERATURE	
AM	**PM**

GROUND CONDITIONS (Wet, Dry, Frozen, Damp)

VISITORS (Name, Company, Reason)

SCHEDULE	PROBLEMS/ DELAYS
Completion Date	
Days Ahead	
Days Behind	

SAFETY ISSUES	ACCIDENTS/ INCIDENTS (Who, Where, When, Contact)

SUMMARY OF WORK PERFORMED TODAY

SIGNATURE		TITLE

EMPLOYEE	Craft	Contracted Hrs.	Overtime		Subcontractors	Craft	Hours Worked

EQUIPMENT ON SITE	No. Units	Working	
		Yes	No

MATERIALS DELIVERED	No. Units	Materials Rented	From & Rate

NOTES

DATE	/	/	**DAY**	M	T	W	T	F	S	Su
FOREMAN										

PROJECT/ JOB		CONTRACT No.	

WEATHER (Hot, Rain, Windy etc.)	**SAFETY MEETING**		

	YES	NO	Subject:

CONCERNS/ ACTIONS:

TEMPERATURE	
AM	**PM**

GROUND CONDITIONS (Wet, Dry, Frozen, Damp)

VISITORS (Name, Company, Reason)

SCHEDULE	**PROBLEMS/ DELAYS**
Completion Date	
Days Ahead	
Days Behind	

SAFETY ISSUES	**ACCIDENTS/ INCIDENTS** (Who, Where, When, Contact)

SUMMARY OF WORK PERFORMED TODAY

SIGNATURE	TITLE

EMPLOYEE	Craft	Contracted Hrs.	Overtime		Subcontractors	Craft	Hours Worked

EQUIPMENT ON SITE	No. Units	Working	
		Yes	No

MATERIALS DELIVERED	No. Units	Materials Rented	From & Rate

NOTES

DATE	/ /	**DAY** M T W T F S Su

FOREMAN	

PROJECT/ JOB		CONTRACT No.	

WEATHER (Hot, Rain, Windy etc.)	**SAFETY MEETING**		
	YES	NO	Subject:

CONCERNS/ ACTIONS:

TEMPERATURE	
AM	**PM**

GROUND CONDITIONS
(Wet, Dry, Frozen, Damp)

VISITORS (Name, Company, Reason)

SCHEDULE		PROBLEMS/ DELAYS
Completion Date		
Days Ahead		
Days Behind		

SAFETY ISSUES	ACCIDENTS/ INCIDENTS (Who, Where, When, Contact)

SUMMARY OF WORK PERFORMED TODAY

SIGNATURE		TITLE	

EMPLOYEE	Craft	Contracted Hrs.	Overtime		Subcontractors	Craft	Hours Worked

EQUIPMENT ON SITE	No. Units	Working	
		Yes	No

MATERIALS DELIVERED	No. Units	Materials Rented	From & Rate

NOTES

DATE	/ /	**DAY** M T W T F S Su
FOREMAN		
PROJECT/ JOB		CONTRACT No.

WEATHER (Hot, Rain, Windy etc.)	**SAFETY MEETING**	

WEATHER
(Hot, Rain, Windy etc.)

SAFETY MEETING

YES	NO	Subject:

CONCERNS/ ACTIONS:

TEMPERATURE

AM	PM

GROUND CONDITIONS
(Wet, Dry, Frozen, Damp)

VISITORS (Name, Company, Reason)

SCHEDULE

Completion Date	
Days Ahead	
Days Behind	

PROBLEMS/ DELAYS

SAFETY ISSUES

ACCIDENTS/ INCIDENTS (Who, Where, When, Contact)

SUMMARY OF WORK PERFORMED TODAY

SIGNATURE		TITLE

EMPLOYEE	Craft	Contracted Hrs.	Overtime		Subcontractors	Craft	Hours Worked

EQUIPMENT ON SITE	No. Units	Working	
		Yes	No

MATERIALS DELIVERED	No. Units	Materials Rented	From & Rate

NOTES

DATE	/	/	**DAY**	M	T	W	T	F	S	Su

FOREMAN	

PROJECT/ JOB		CONTRACT No.	

WEATHER (Hot, Rain, Windy etc.)	**SAFETY MEETING**		

	YES	NO	Subject:

CONCERNS/ ACTIONS:

TEMPERATURE

AM	**PM**

GROUND CONDITIONS
(Wet, Dry, Frozen, Damp)

VISITORS (Name, Company, Reason)

SCHEDULE

Completion Date	
Days Ahead	
Days Behind	

PROBLEMS/ DELAYS

SAFETY ISSUES

ACCIDENTS/ INCIDENTS (Who, Where, When, Contact)

SUMMARY OF WORK PERFORMED TODAY

SIGNATURE	TITLE

EMPLOYEE	Craft	Contracted Hrs.	Overtime	Subcontractors	Craft	Hours Worked

EQUIPMENT ON SITE	No. Units	Working Yes	No

MATERIALS DELIVERED	No. Units	Materials Rented	From & Rate

NOTES

DATE	/	/	**DAY**	M	T	W	T	F	S	Su

FOREMAN	

PROJECT/ JOB		**CONTRACT No.**	

WEATHER (Hot, Rain, Windy etc.)	**SAFETY MEETING**		

	YES	NO	Subject:

CONCERNS/ ACTIONS:

TEMPERATURE	
AM	**PM**

GROUND CONDITIONS (Wet, Dry, Frozen, Damp)	**VISITORS** (Name, Company, Reason)

SCHEDULE	**PROBLEMS/ DELAYS**
Completion Date	
Days Ahead	
Days Behind	

SAFETY ISSUES	**ACCIDENTS/ INCIDENTS** (Who, Where, When, Contact)

SUMMARY OF WORK PERFORMED TODAY

SIGNATURE		TITLE	

EMPLOYEE	Craft	Contracted Hrs.	Overtime		Subcontractors	Craft	Hours Worked

EQUIPMENT ON SITE	No. Units	Working	
		Yes	No

MATERIALS DELIVERED	No. Units	Materials Rented	From & Rate

NOTES

DATE	/ /	**DAY**	M	T	W	T	F	S	Su

FOREMAN	

PROJECT/ JOB		CONTRACT No.	

WEATHER (Hot, Rain, Windy etc.)	**SAFETY MEETING**		
	YES	NO	Subject:
	CONCERNS/ ACTIONS:		

TEMPERATURE

AM	PM

GROUND CONDITIONS (Wet, Dry, Frozen, Damp)	**VISITORS** (Name, Company, Reason)

SCHEDULE — **PROBLEMS/ DELAYS**

Completion Date	
Days Ahead	
Days Behind	

SAFETY ISSUES — **ACCIDENTS/ INCIDENTS** (Who, Where, When, Contact)

SUMMARY OF WORK PERFORMED TODAY

SIGNATURE		TITLE	

EMPLOYEE	Craft	Contracted Hrs.	Overtime	Subcontractors	Craft	Hours Worked

EQUIPMENT ON SITE	No. Units	Working	
		Yes	No

MATERIALS DELIVERED	No. Units	Materials Rented	From & Rate

NOTES

DATE	/ /	**DAY**	M	T	W	T	F	S	Su

FOREMAN	

PROJECT/ JOB		**CONTRACT No.**	

WEATHER (Hot, Rain, Windy etc.)	**SAFETY MEETING**		
	YES	NO	Subject:
	CONCERNS/ ACTIONS:		

TEMPERATURE	
AM	**PM**

GROUND CONDITIONS (Wet, Dry, Frozen, Damp)

VISITORS (Name, Company, Reason)

SCHEDULE	
Completion Date	
Days Ahead	
Days Behind	

PROBLEMS/ DELAYS

SAFETY ISSUES

ACCIDENTS/ INCIDENTS (Who, Where, When, Contact)

SUMMARY OF WORK PERFORMED TODAY

SIGNATURE		TITLE	

EMPLOYEE	Craft	Contracted Hrs.	Overtime		Subcontractors	Craft	Hours Worked

EQUIPMENT ON SITE	No. Units	Working	
		Yes	No

MATERIALS DELIVERED	No. Units	Materials Rented	From & Rate

NOTES

_____
_____
_____
_____
_____
_____

DATE	/	/	**DAY**	M	T	W	T	F	S	Su
FOREMAN										
PROJECT/ JOB			**CONTRACT No.**							

WEATHER (Hot, Rain, Windy etc.)	**SAFETY MEETING**				

SAFETY MEETING

YES	NO	Subject:

CONCERNS/ ACTIONS:

TEMPERATURE

AM	PM

GROUND CONDITIONS
(Wet, Dry, Frozen, Damp)

VISITORS (Name, Company, Reason)

SCHEDULE

Completion Date	
Days Ahead	
Days Behind	

PROBLEMS/ DELAYS

SAFETY ISSUES

ACCIDENTS/ INCIDENTS (Who, Where, When, Contact)

SUMMARY OF WORK PERFORMED TODAY

SIGNATURE	TITLE

EMPLOYEE	Craft	Contracted Hrs.	Overtime	Subcontractors	Craft	Hours Worked

EQUIPMENT ON SITE	No. Units	Working	
		Yes	No

MATERIALS DELIVERED	No. Units	Materials Rented	From & Rate

NOTES

DATE	/	/	DAY	M	T	W	T	F	S	Su

FOREMAN	

PROJECT/ JOB		CONTRACT No.	

WEATHER
(Hot, Rain, Windy etc.)

SAFETY MEETING

YES	NO	Subject:

CONCERNS/ ACTIONS:

TEMPERATURE

AM	PM

GROUND CONDITIONS
(Wet, Dry, Frozen, Damp)

VISITORS (Name, Company, Reason)

SCHEDULE

Completion Date	
Days Ahead	
Days Behind	

PROBLEMS/ DELAYS

SAFETY ISSUES

ACCIDENTS/ INCIDENTS (Who, Where, When, Contact)

SUMMARY OF WORK PERFORMED TODAY

SIGNATURE		TITLE	

EMPLOYEE	Craft	Contracted Hrs.	Overtime		Subcontractors	Craft	Hours Worked

EQUIPMENT ON SITE	No. Units	Working	
		Yes	No

MATERIALS DELIVERED	No. Units	Materials Rented	From & Rate

NOTES

DATE	/ /	**DAY** M T W T F S Su
FOREMAN		
PROJECT/ JOB		CONTRACT No.

WEATHER (Hot, Rain, Windy etc.)	**SAFETY MEETING**		
	YES	NO	Subject:

CONCERNS/ ACTIONS:

TEMPERATURE	
AM	**PM**

GROUND CONDITIONS (Wet, Dry, Frozen, Damp)

VISITORS (Name, Company, Reason)

SCHEDULE	
Completion Date	
Days Ahead	
Days Behind	

PROBLEMS/ DELAYS

SAFETY ISSUES

ACCIDENTS/ INCIDENTS (Who, Where, When, Contact)

SUMMARY OF WORK PERFORMED TODAY

SIGNATURE		TITLE

EMPLOYEE	Craft	Contracted Hrs.	Overtime		Subcontractors	Craft	Hours Worked

EQUIPMENT ON SITE	No. Units	Working	
		Yes	No

MATERIALS DELIVERED	No. Units	Materials Rented	From & Rate

NOTES

DATE	/	/	**DAY**	M	T	W	T	F	S	Su

FOREMAN	

PROJECT/ JOB		CONTRACT No.	

WEATHER (Hot, Rain, Windy etc.)	**SAFETY MEETING**		
	YES	NO	Subject:

CONCERNS/ ACTIONS:

TEMPERATURE	
AM	**PM**

GROUND CONDITIONS (Wet, Dry, Frozen, Damp)	**VISITORS** (Name, Company, Reason)

SCHEDULE		**PROBLEMS/ DELAYS**
Completion Date		
Days Ahead		
Days Behind		

SAFETY ISSUES	**ACCIDENTS/ INCIDENTS** (Who, Where, When, Contact)

SUMMARY OF WORK PERFORMED TODAY

SIGNATURE	TITLE

EMPLOYEE	Craft	Contracted Hrs.	Overtime		Subcontractors	Craft	Hours Worked

EQUIPMENT ON SITE	No. Units	Working	
		Yes	No

MATERIALS DELIVERED	No. Units	Materials Rented	From & Rate

NOTES

DATE	/ /	**DAY**	M	T	W	T	F	S	Su

FOREMAN	
PROJECT/ JOB		CONTRACT No.	

WEATHER (Hot, Rain, Windy etc.)	**SAFETY MEETING**		
	YES	NO	Subject:
	CONCERNS/ ACTIONS:		

TEMPERATURE	
AM	**PM**

GROUND CONDITIONS (Wet, Dry, Frozen, Damp)

VISITORS (Name, Company, Reason)

SCHEDULE	
Completion Date	
Days Ahead	
Days Behind	

PROBLEMS/ DELAYS

SAFETY ISSUES

ACCIDENTS/ INCIDENTS (Who, Where, When, Contact)

SUMMARY OF WORK PERFORMED TODAY

SIGNATURE		TITLE

EMPLOYEE	Craft	Contracted Hrs.	Overtime		Subcontractors	Craft	Hours Worked

EQUIPMENT ON SITE	No. Units	Working	
		Yes	No

MATERIALS DELIVERED	No. Units	Materials Rented	From & Rate

NOTES

DATE	/ /	**DAY**	M	T	W	T	F	S	Su
FOREMAN									

PROJECT/ JOB		CONTRACT No.	

WEATHER (Hot, Rain, Windy etc.)	**SAFETY MEETING**		

	YES	NO	Subject:

CONCERNS/ ACTIONS:

TEMPERATURE	
AM	**PM**

GROUND CONDITIONS
(Wet, Dry, Frozen, Damp)

VISITORS (Name, Company, Reason)

SCHEDULE	PROBLEMS/ DELAYS
Completion Date	
Days Ahead	
Days Behind	

SAFETY ISSUES	ACCIDENTS/ INCIDENTS (Who, Where, When, Contact)

SUMMARY OF WORK PERFORMED TODAY

SIGNATURE	TITLE

EMPLOYEE	Craft	Contracted Hrs.	Overtime		Subcontractors	Craft	Hours Worked

EQUIPMENT ON SITE	No. Units	Working	
		Yes	No

MATERIALS DELIVERED	No. Units	Materials Rented	From & Rate

NOTES

DATE	/	/	**DAY**	M	T	W	T	F	S	Su
FOREMAN										
PROJECT/ JOB			CONTRACT No.							

WEATHER (Hot, Rain, Windy etc.)	**SAFETY MEETING**		
	YES	NO	Subject:
	CONCERNS/ ACTIONS:		

TEMPERATURE	
AM	**PM**

GROUND CONDITIONS
(Wet, Dry, Frozen, Damp)

VISITORS (Name, Company, Reason)

SCHEDULE		**PROBLEMS/ DELAYS**
Completion Date		
Days Ahead		
Days Behind		

SAFETY ISSUES	**ACCIDENTS/ INCIDENTS** (Who, Where, When, Contact)

SUMMARY OF WORK PERFORMED TODAY

SIGNATURE	TITLE

EMPLOYEE	Craft	Contracted Hrs.	Overtime		Subcontractors	Craft	Hours Worked

EQUIPMENT ON SITE	No. Units	Working	
		Yes	No

MATERIALS DELIVERED	No. Units	Materials Rented	From & Rate

NOTES

DATE	/ /	**DAY**	M	T	W	T	F	S	Su

FOREMAN

PROJECT/ JOB		CONTRACT No.	

WEATHER (Hot, Rain, Windy etc.)	**SAFETY MEETING**

	YES	NO	Subject:

CONCERNS/ ACTIONS:

TEMPERATURE

AM	**PM**

GROUND CONDITIONS
(Wet, Dry, Frozen, Damp)

VISITORS (Name, Company, Reason)

SCHEDULE

PROBLEMS/ DELAYS

Completion Date	
Days Ahead	
Days Behind	

SAFETY ISSUES

ACCIDENTS/ INCIDENTS (Who, Where, When, Contact)

SUMMARY OF WORK PERFORMED TODAY

SIGNATURE		TITLE	

EMPLOYEE	Craft	Contracted Hrs.	Overtime		Subcontractors	Craft	Hours Worked

EQUIPMENT ON SITE	No. Units	Working	
		Yes	No

MATERIALS DELIVERED	No. Units	Materials Rented	From & Rate

NOTES

DATE	/ /	**DAY** M T W T F S Su

FOREMAN	

PROJECT/ JOB		**CONTRACT No.**	

WEATHER (Hot, Rain, Windy etc.)	**SAFETY MEETING**

YES	NO	Subject:

CONCERNS/ ACTIONS:

TEMPERATURE	
AM	**PM**

GROUND CONDITIONS (Wet, Dry, Frozen, Damp)

VISITORS (Name, Company, Reason)

SCHEDULE	
Completion Date	
Days Ahead	
Days Behind	

PROBLEMS/ DELAYS

SAFETY ISSUES

ACCIDENTS/ INCIDENTS (Who, Where, When, Contact)

SUMMARY OF WORK PERFORMED TODAY

SIGNATURE	**TITLE**

EMPLOYEE	Craft	Contracted Hrs.	Overtime		Subcontractors	Craft	Hours Worked

EQUIPMENT ON SITE	No. Units	Working	
		Yes	No

MATERIALS DELIVERED	No. Units	Materials Rented	From & Rate

NOTES

DATE	/ /	**DAY**	M	T	W	T	F	S	Su

FOREMAN	
PROJECT/ JOB		CONTRACT No.	

WEATHER (Hot, Rain, Windy etc.)	**SAFETY MEETING**		
	YES	NO	Subject:

CONCERNS/ ACTIONS:

TEMPERATURE	
AM	**PM**

GROUND CONDITIONS (Wet, Dry, Frozen, Damp)

VISITORS (Name, Company, Reason)

SCHEDULE

Completion Date	
Days Ahead	
Days Behind	

PROBLEMS/ DELAYS

SAFETY ISSUES

ACCIDENTS/ INCIDENTS (Who, Where, When, Contact)

SUMMARY OF WORK PERFORMED TODAY

SIGNATURE		TITLE

EMPLOYEE	Craft	Contracted Hrs.	Overtime		Subcontractors	Craft	Hours Worked

EQUIPMENT ON SITE	No. Units	Working	
		Yes	No

MATERIALS DELIVERED	No. Units	Materials Rented	From & Rate

NOTES

DATE	/ /	**DAY**	M	T	W	T	F	S	Su

FOREMAN	
PROJECT/ JOB		CONTRACT No.	

WEATHER (Hot, Rain, Windy etc.)	**SAFETY MEETING**		
	YES	NO	Subject:
	CONCERNS/ ACTIONS:		

TEMPERATURE

AM	PM

GROUND CONDITIONS (Wet, Dry, Frozen, Damp)

VISITORS (Name, Company, Reason)

SCHEDULE

PROBLEMS/ DELAYS

Completion Date	
Days Ahead	
Days Behind	

SAFETY ISSUES

ACCIDENTS/ INCIDENTS (Who, Where, When, Contact)

SUMMARY OF WORK PERFORMED TODAY

SIGNATURE		TITLE	

EMPLOYEE	Craft	Contracted Hrs.	Overtime		Subcontractors	Craft	Hours Worked

EQUIPMENT ON SITE	No. Units	Working	
		Yes	No

MATERIALS DELIVERED	No. Units	Materials Rented	From & Rate

NOTES

DATE	/ /	**DAY**	M	T	W	T	F	S	Su

FOREMAN	

PROJECT/ JOB		**CONTRACT No.**	

WEATHER (Hot, Rain, Windy etc.)	**SAFETY MEETING**		
	YES	**NO**	**Subject:**

CONCERNS/ ACTIONS:

TEMPERATURE	
AM	**PM**

GROUND CONDITIONS
(Wet, Dry, Frozen, Damp)

VISITORS (Name, Company, Reason)

SCHEDULE	
Completion Date	
Days Ahead	
Days Behind	

PROBLEMS/ DELAYS

SAFETY ISSUES

ACCIDENTS/ INCIDENTS (Who, Where, When, Contact)

SUMMARY OF WORK PERFORMED TODAY

SIGNATURE	**TITLE**

EMPLOYEE	Craft	Contracted Hrs.	Overtime		Subcontractors	Craft	Hours Worked

EQUIPMENT ON SITE	No. Units	Working	
		Yes	No

MATERIALS DELIVERED	No. Units	Materials Rented	From & Rate

NOTES

| DATE | / | / | DAY | M | T | W | T | F | S | Su |

| FOREMAN | |

| PROJECT/ JOB | | CONTRACT No. | |

| WEATHER (Hot, Rain, Windy etc.) | SAFETY MEETING |

| | YES | NO | Subject: |

CONCERNS/ ACTIONS:

TEMPERATURE

AM	PM

GROUND CONDITIONS
(Wet, Dry, Frozen, Damp)

VISITORS (Name, Company, Reason)

SCHEDULE

Completion Date	
Days Ahead	
Days Behind	

PROBLEMS/ DELAYS

SAFETY ISSUES

ACCIDENTS/ INCIDENTS (Who, Where, When, Contact)

SUMMARY OF WORK PERFORMED TODAY

| SIGNATURE | | TITLE |

EMPLOYEE	Craft	Contracted Hrs.	Overtime		Subcontractors	Craft	Hours Worked

EQUIPMENT ON SITE	No. Units	Working	
		Yes	No

MATERIALS DELIVERED	No. Units	Materials Rented	From & Rate

NOTES

DATE	/ /	**DAY**	M	T	W	T	F	S	Su

FOREMAN	

PROJECT/ JOB		CONTRACT No.	

WEATHER
(Hot, Rain, Windy etc.)

SAFETY MEETING

YES	NO	Subject:

CONCERNS/ ACTIONS:

TEMPERATURE

AM	PM

GROUND CONDITIONS
(Wet, Dry, Frozen, Damp)

VISITORS (Name, Company, Reason)

SCHEDULE

Completion Date	
Days Ahead	
Days Behind	

PROBLEMS/ DELAYS

SAFETY ISSUES

ACCIDENTS/ INCIDENTS (Who, Where, When, Contact)

SUMMARY OF WORK PERFORMED TODAY

SIGNATURE		TITLE

EMPLOYEE	Craft	Contracted Hrs.	Overtime		Subcontractors	Craft	Hours Worked

EQUIPMENT ON SITE	No. Units	Working	
		Yes	No

MATERIALS DELIVERED	No. Units	Materials Rented	From & Rate

NOTES

DATE	/ /	**DAY**	M	T	W	T	F	S	Su
FOREMAN									
PROJECT/ JOB		CONTRACT No.							

WEATHER (Hot, Rain, Windy etc.)	**SAFETY MEETING**		
	YES	NO	Subject:

CONCERNS/ ACTIONS:

TEMPERATURE	
AM	**PM**

GROUND CONDITIONS (Wet, Dry, Frozen, Damp)

VISITORS (Name, Company, Reason)

SCHEDULE	
Completion Date	
Days Ahead	
Days Behind	

PROBLEMS/ DELAYS

SAFETY ISSUES

ACCIDENTS/ INCIDENTS (Who, Where, When, Contact)

SUMMARY OF WORK PERFORMED TODAY

SIGNATURE	TITLE

EMPLOYEE	Craft	Contracted Hrs.	Overtime		Subcontractors	Craft	Hours Worked

EQUIPMENT ON SITE	No. Units	Working	
		Yes	No

MATERIALS DELIVERED	No. Units	Materials Rented	From & Rate

NOTES

DATE	/	/	**DAY**	M	T	W	T	F	S	Su

FOREMAN	

PROJECT/ JOB		CONTRACT No.	

WEATHER (Hot, Rain, Windy etc.)	**SAFETY MEETING**		
	YES	NO	Subject:
	CONCERNS/ ACTIONS:		

TEMPERATURE	
AM	**PM**

GROUND CONDITIONS (Wet, Dry, Frozen, Damp)	VISITORS (Name, Company, Reason)

SCHEDULE		PROBLEMS/ DELAYS
Completion Date		
Days Ahead		
Days Behind		

SAFETY ISSUES	ACCIDENTS/ INCIDENTS (Who, Where, When, Contact)

SUMMARY OF WORK PERFORMED TODAY

SIGNATURE	TITLE

EMPLOYEE	Craft	Contracted Hrs.	Overtime		Subcontractors	Craft	Hours Worked

EQUIPMENT ON SITE	No. Units	Working	
		Yes	No

MATERIALS DELIVERED	No. Units	Materials Rented	From & Rate

NOTES

DATE	/ /	**DAY**	M	T	W	T	F	S	Su

FOREMAN	
PROJECT/ JOB		CONTRACT No.	

WEATHER (Hot, Rain, Windy etc.)		**SAFETY MEETING**		
		YES	NO	Subject:
		CONCERNS/ ACTIONS:		

TEMPERATURE

AM	PM

GROUND CONDITIONS (Wet, Dry, Frozen, Damp)

VISITORS (Name, Company, Reason)

SCHEDULE

Completion Date	
Days Ahead	
Days Behind	

PROBLEMS/ DELAYS

SAFETY ISSUES

ACCIDENTS/ INCIDENTS (Who, Where, When, Contact)

SUMMARY OF WORK PERFORMED TODAY

SIGNATURE		TITLE	

EMPLOYEE	Craft	Contracted Hrs.	Overtime		Subcontractors	Craft	Hours Worked

EQUIPMENT ON SITE	No. Units	Working	
		Yes	No

MATERIALS DELIVERED	No. Units	Materials Rented	From & Rate

NOTES

DATE	/ /	**DAY**	M	T	W	T	F	S	Su

FOREMAN	
PROJECT/ JOB		CONTRACT No.	

WEATHER (Hot, Rain, Windy etc.)	**SAFETY MEETING**

	YES	NO	Subject:

CONCERNS/ ACTIONS:

TEMPERATURE	
AM	**PM**

GROUND CONDITIONS (Wet, Dry, Frozen, Damp)	**VISITORS** (Name, Company, Reason)

SCHEDULE		**PROBLEMS/ DELAYS**
Completion Date		
Days Ahead		
Days Behind		

SAFETY ISSUES	**ACCIDENTS/ INCIDENTS** (Who, Where, When, Contact)

SUMMARY OF WORK PERFORMED TODAY

SIGNATURE	TITLE

EMPLOYEE	Craft	Contracted Hrs.	Overtime		Subcontractors	Craft	Hours Worked

EQUIPMENT ON SITE	No. Units	Working	
		Yes	No

MATERIALS DELIVERED	No. Units	Materials Rented	From & Rate

NOTES

DATE	/ /	**DAY**	M	T	W	T	F	S	Su

FOREMAN	
PROJECT/ JOB		CONTRACT No.	

WEATHER (Hot, Rain, Windy etc.)	**SAFETY MEETING**		
	YES	NO	Subject:

CONCERNS/ ACTIONS:

TEMPERATURE	
AM	**PM**

GROUND CONDITIONS (Wet, Dry, Frozen, Damp)

VISITORS (Name, Company, Reason)

SCHEDULE	**PROBLEMS/ DELAYS**
Completion Date	
Days Ahead	
Days Behind	

SAFETY ISSUES	**ACCIDENTS/ INCIDENTS** (Who, Where, When, Contact)

SUMMARY OF WORK PERFORMED TODAY

SIGNATURE		TITLE	

EMPLOYEE	Craft	Contracted Hrs.	Overtime	Subcontractors	Craft	Hours Worked

EQUIPMENT ON SITE	No. Units	Working	
		Yes	No

MATERIALS DELIVERED	No. Units	Materials Rented	From & Rate

NOTES

DATE	/ /	**DAY**	M	T	W	T	F	S	Su

FOREMAN	

PROJECT/ JOB		CONTRACT No.	

WEATHER
(Hot, Rain, Windy etc.)

SAFETY MEETING

YES	NO	Subject:

CONCERNS/ ACTIONS:

TEMPERATURE

AM	PM

GROUND CONDITIONS
(Wet, Dry, Frozen, Damp)

VISITORS (Name, Company, Reason)

SCHEDULE

Completion Date	
Days Ahead	
Days Behind	

PROBLEMS/ DELAYS

SAFETY ISSUES

ACCIDENTS/ INCIDENTS (Who, Where, When, Contact)

SUMMARY OF WORK PERFORMED TODAY

SIGNATURE		TITLE	

EMPLOYEE	Craft	Contracted Hrs.	Overtime	Subcontractors	Craft	Hours Worked

EQUIPMENT ON SITE	No. Units	Working Yes	Working No

MATERIALS DELIVERED	No. Units	Materials Rented	From & Rate

NOTES

_____
_____
_____
_____
_____
_____
_____

DATE	/ /	**DAY**	M	T	W	T	F	S	Su

FOREMAN	

PROJECT/ JOB		CONTRACT No.	

WEATHER (Hot, Rain, Windy etc.)	**SAFETY MEETING**

		SAFETY MEETING		
YES	NO	Subject:		

CONCERNS/ ACTIONS:

TEMPERATURE

AM	PM

GROUND CONDITIONS (Wet, Dry, Frozen, Damp)

VISITORS (Name, Company, Reason)

SCHEDULE

Completion Date	
Days Ahead	
Days Behind	

PROBLEMS/ DELAYS

SAFETY ISSUES

ACCIDENTS/ INCIDENTS (Who, Where, When, Contact)

SUMMARY OF WORK PERFORMED TODAY

SIGNATURE		TITLE	

EMPLOYEE	Craft	Contracted Hrs.	Overtime		Subcontractors	Craft	Hours Worked

EQUIPMENT ON SITE	No. Units	Working	
		Yes	No

MATERIALS DELIVERED	No. Units	Materials Rented	From & Rate

NOTES

DATE	/ /	**DAY**	M	T	W	T	F	S	Su

FOREMAN	
PROJECT/ JOB	
	CONTRACT No.	

WEATHER
(Hot, Rain, Windy etc.)

SAFETY MEETING

YES	NO	Subject:

CONCERNS/ ACTIONS:

TEMPERATURE

AM	PM

GROUND CONDITIONS
(Wet, Dry, Frozen, Damp)

VISITORS (Name, Company, Reason)

SCHEDULE

Completion Date	
Days Ahead	
Days Behind	

PROBLEMS/ DELAYS

SAFETY ISSUES

ACCIDENTS/ INCIDENTS (Who, Where, When, Contact)

SUMMARY OF WORK PERFORMED TODAY

SIGNATURE		TITLE

EMPLOYEE	Craft	Contracted Hrs.	Overtime	Subcontractors	Craft	Hours Worked

EQUIPMENT ON SITE	No. Units	Working Yes	Working No

MATERIALS DELIVERED	No. Units	Materials Rented	From & Rate

NOTES

_____
_____
_____
_____
_____
_____

DATE	/	/	**DAY**	M	T	W	T	F	S	Su

FOREMAN	
PROJECT/ JOB		CONTRACT No.	

WEATHER (Hot, Rain, Windy etc.)	**SAFETY MEETING**		
	YES	NO	Subject:
	CONCERNS/ ACTIONS:		

TEMPERATURE	
AM	**PM**

VISITORS (Name, Company, Reason)

GROUND CONDITIONS
(Wet, Dry, Frozen, Damp)

SCHEDULE	
Completion Date	
Days Ahead	
Days Behind	

PROBLEMS/ DELAYS

SAFETY ISSUES

ACCIDENTS/ INCIDENTS (Who, Where, When, Contact)

SUMMARY OF WORK PERFORMED TODAY

SIGNATURE		TITLE	

EMPLOYEE	Craft	Contracted Hrs.	Overtime	Subcontractors	Craft	Hours Worked

EQUIPMENT ON SITE	No. Units	Working Yes	Working No

MATERIALS DELIVERED	No. Units	Materials Rented	From & Rate

NOTES

DATE	/ /	**DAY**	M	T	W	T	F	S	Su
FOREMAN									
PROJECT/ JOB		CONTRACT No.							

WEATHER (Hot, Rain, Windy etc.)	**SAFETY MEETING**		
	YES	NO	Subject:

CONCERNS/ ACTIONS:

TEMPERATURE	
AM	**PM**

GROUND CONDITIONS
(Wet, Dry, Frozen, Damp)

VISITORS (Name, Company, Reason)

SCHEDULE	
Completion Date	
Days Ahead	
Days Behind	

PROBLEMS/ DELAYS

SAFETY ISSUES

ACCIDENTS/ INCIDENTS (Who, Where, When, Contact)

SUMMARY OF WORK PERFORMED TODAY

SIGNATURE	TITLE

EMPLOYEE	Craft	Contracted Hrs.	Overtime	Subcontractors	Craft	Hours Worked

EQUIPMENT ON SITE	No. Units	Working	
		Yes	No

MATERIALS DELIVERED	No. Units	Materials Rented	From & Rate

NOTES

DATE	/ /	**DAY**	M T W T F S Su

FOREMAN	

PROJECT/ JOB		CONTRACT No.	

WEATHER (Hot, Rain, Windy etc.)	**SAFETY MEETING**

SAFETY MEETING		
YES	NO	Subject:

CONCERNS/ ACTIONS:

TEMPERATURE

AM	PM

GROUND CONDITIONS
(Wet, Dry, Frozen, Damp)

VISITORS (Name, Company, Reason)

SCHEDULE

Completion Date	
Days Ahead	
Days Behind	

PROBLEMS/ DELAYS

SAFETY ISSUES

ACCIDENTS/ INCIDENTS (Who, Where, When, Contact)

SUMMARY OF WORK PERFORMED TODAY

SIGNATURE		TITLE

EMPLOYEE	Craft	Contracted Hrs.	Overtime	Subcontractors	Craft	Hours Worked

EQUIPMENT ON SITE	No. Units	Working Yes	No

MATERIALS DELIVERED	No. Units	Materials Rented	From & Rate

NOTES

DATE	/ /	**DAY** M T W T F S Su
FOREMAN		
PROJECT/ JOB		CONTRACT No.	

WEATHER (Hot, Rain, Windy etc.)	**SAFETY MEETING**		

	YES	NO	Subject:

CONCERNS/ ACTIONS:

TEMPERATURE	
AM	**PM**

GROUND CONDITIONS (Wet, Dry, Frozen, Damp)

VISITORS (Name, Company, Reason)

SCHEDULE	
Completion Date	
Days Ahead	
Days Behind	

PROBLEMS/ DELAYS

SAFETY ISSUES

ACCIDENTS/ INCIDENTS (Who, Where, When, Contact)

SUMMARY OF WORK PERFORMED TODAY

SIGNATURE		TITLE	

EMPLOYEE	Craft	Contracted Hrs.	Overtime	Subcontractors	Craft	Hours Worked

EQUIPMENT ON SITE	No. Units	Working	
		Yes	No

MATERIALS DELIVERED	No. Units	Materials Rented	From & Rate

NOTES

DATE	/ /	**DAY**	M	T	W	T	F	S	Su

FOREMAN

PROJECT/ JOB		CONTRACT No.	

WEATHER
(Hot, Rain, Windy etc.)

TEMPERATURE

AM	PM

GROUND CONDITIONS
(Wet, Dry, Frozen, Damp)

SCHEDULE

Completion Date	
Days Ahead	
Days Behind	

SAFETY ISSUES

SAFETY MEETING

YES	NO	Subject:

CONCERNS/ ACTIONS:

VISITORS (Name, Company, Reason)

PROBLEMS/ DELAYS

ACCIDENTS/ INCIDENTS (Who, Where, When, Contact)

SUMMARY OF WORK PERFORMED TODAY

SIGNATURE	TITLE

EMPLOYEE	Craft	Contracted Hrs.	Overtime		Subcontractors	Craft	Hours Worked

EQUIPMENT ON SITE	No. Units	Working	
		Yes	No

MATERIALS DELIVERED	No. Units	Materials Rented	From & Rate

NOTES

DATE	/ /	**DAY**	M	T	W	T	F	S	Su

FOREMAN	

PROJECT/ JOB		CONTRACT No.	

WEATHER
(Hot, Rain, Windy etc.)

SAFETY MEETING

YES	NO	Subject:

CONCERNS/ ACTIONS:

TEMPERATURE

AM	PM

GROUND CONDITIONS
(Wet, Dry, Frozen, Damp)

VISITORS (Name, Company, Reason)

SCHEDULE

Completion Date	
Days Ahead	
Days Behind	

PROBLEMS/ DELAYS

SAFETY ISSUES

ACCIDENTS/ INCIDENTS (Who, Where, When, Contact)

SUMMARY OF WORK PERFORMED TODAY

SIGNATURE		TITLE	

EMPLOYEE	Craft	Contracted Hrs.	Overtime		Subcontractors	Craft	Hours Worked

EQUIPMENT ON SITE	No. Units	Working	
		Yes	No

MATERIALS DELIVERED	No. Units	Materials Rented	From & Rate

NOTES

DATE	/ /	**DAY** M T W T F S Su

FOREMAN	

PROJECT/ JOB		**CONTRACT No.**	

WEATHER (Hot, Rain, Windy etc.)	**SAFETY MEETING**		
	YES	NO	Subject:
	CONCERNS/ ACTIONS:		

TEMPERATURE

AM	PM

GROUND CONDITIONS (Wet, Dry, Frozen, Damp)	**VISITORS** (Name, Company, Reason)

SCHEDULE	**PROBLEMS/ DELAYS**
Completion Date	
Days Ahead	
Days Behind	

SAFETY ISSUES	**ACCIDENTS/ INCIDENTS** (Who, Where, When, Contact)

SUMMARY OF WORK PERFORMED TODAY

SIGNATURE	TITLE

EMPLOYEE	Craft	Contracted Hrs.	Overtime		Subcontractors	Craft	Hours Worked

EQUIPMENT ON SITE	No. Units	Working	
		Yes	No

MATERIALS DELIVERED	No. Units	Materials Rented	From & Rate

NOTES

DATE	/ /	**DAY**	M T W T F S Su

FOREMAN	

PROJECT/ JOB		CONTRACT No.	

WEATHER (Hot, Rain, Windy etc.)	**SAFETY MEETING**

	YES	NO	Subject:

CONCERNS/ ACTIONS:

TEMPERATURE	
AM	**PM**

GROUND CONDITIONS (Wet, Dry, Frozen, Damp)

VISITORS (Name, Company, Reason)

SCHEDULE	
Completion Date	
Days Ahead	
Days Behind	

PROBLEMS/ DELAYS

SAFETY ISSUES

ACCIDENTS/ INCIDENTS (Who, Where, When, Contact)

SUMMARY OF WORK PERFORMED TODAY

SIGNATURE		TITLE

EMPLOYEE	Craft	Contracted Hrs.	Overtime		Subcontractors	Craft	Hours Worked

EQUIPMENT ON SITE	No. Units	Working	
		Yes	No

MATERIALS DELIVERED	No. Units	Materials Rented	From & Rate

NOTES
_____
_____
_____
_____
_____
_____

DATE	/ /	**DAY**	M	T	W	T	F	S	Su

FOREMAN	
PROJECT/ JOB		CONTRACT No.	

WEATHER (Hot, Rain, Windy etc.)	**SAFETY MEETING**		

	YES	NO	Subject:

CONCERNS/ ACTIONS:

TEMPERATURE	
AM	**PM**

GROUND CONDITIONS (Wet, Dry, Frozen, Damp)	VISITORS (Name, Company, Reason)

SCHEDULE		PROBLEMS/ DELAYS
Completion Date		
Days Ahead		
Days Behind		

SAFETY ISSUES	ACCIDENTS/ INCIDENTS (Who, Where, When, Contact)

SUMMARY OF WORK PERFORMED TODAY

SIGNATURE	TITLE

EMPLOYEE	Craft	Contracted Hrs.	Overtime	Subcontractors	Craft	Hours Worked

EQUIPMENT ON SITE	No. Units	Working	
		Yes	No

MATERIALS DELIVERED	No. Units	Materials Rented	From & Rate

NOTES

DATE	/ /	**DAY**	M	T	W	T	F	S	Su

FOREMAN

PROJECT/ JOB		CONTRACT No.	

WEATHER (Hot, Rain, Windy etc.)	**SAFETY MEETING**		
	YES	NO	Subject:
	CONCERNS/ ACTIONS:		

TEMPERATURE

AM	PM

GROUND CONDITIONS (Wet, Dry, Frozen, Damp)

VISITORS (Name, Company, Reason)

SCHEDULE

PROBLEMS/ DELAYS

Completion Date	
Days Ahead	
Days Behind	

SAFETY ISSUES

ACCIDENTS/ INCIDENTS (Who, Where, When, Contact)

SUMMARY OF WORK PERFORMED TODAY

SIGNATURE	TITLE

EMPLOYEE	Craft	Contracted Hrs.	Overtime		Subcontractors	Craft	Hours Worked

EQUIPMENT ON SITE	No. Units	Working	
		Yes	No

MATERIALS DELIVERED	No. Units	Materials Rented	From & Rate

NOTES

DATE	/ /	**DAY**	M	T	W	T	F	S	Su

FOREMAN	
PROJECT/ JOB		CONTRACT No.	

WEATHER (Hot, Rain, Windy etc.)	**SAFETY MEETING**		
	YES	NO	Subject:

CONCERNS/ ACTIONS:

TEMPERATURE	
AM	**PM**

GROUND CONDITIONS (Wet, Dry, Frozen, Damp)

VISITORS (Name, Company, Reason)

SCHEDULE	
Completion Date	
Days Ahead	
Days Behind	

PROBLEMS/ DELAYS

SAFETY ISSUES

ACCIDENTS/ INCIDENTS (Who, Where, When, Contact)

SUMMARY OF WORK PERFORMED TODAY

SIGNATURE		TITLE	

EMPLOYEE	Craft	Contracted Hrs.	Overtime		Subcontractors	Craft	Hours Worked

EQUIPMENT ON SITE	No. Units	Working	
		Yes	No

MATERIALS DELIVERED	No. Units	Materials Rented	From & Rate

NOTES

DATE	/	/	**DAY**	M	T	W	T	F	S	Su

FOREMAN	

PROJECT/ JOB		CONTRACT No.	

WEATHER (Hot, Rain, Windy etc.)	**SAFETY MEETING**		
	YES	NO	Subject:

CONCERNS/ ACTIONS:

TEMPERATURE	
AM	**PM**

GROUND CONDITIONS (Wet, Dry, Frozen, Damp)

VISITORS (Name, Company, Reason)

SCHEDULE	
Completion Date	
Days Ahead	
Days Behind	

PROBLEMS/ DELAYS

SAFETY ISSUES

ACCIDENTS/ INCIDENTS (Who, Where, When, Contact)

SUMMARY OF WORK PERFORMED TODAY

SIGNATURE	TITLE

EMPLOYEE	Craft	Contracted Hrs.	Overtime		Subcontractors	Craft	Hours Worked

EQUIPMENT ON SITE	No. Units	Working	
		Yes	No

MATERIALS DELIVERED	No. Units	Materials Rented	From & Rate

NOTES

DATE	/ /	**DAY**	M	T	W	T	F	S	Su

FOREMAN	
PROJECT/ JOB		CONTRACT No.	

WEATHER (Hot, Rain, Windy etc.)	**SAFETY MEETING**

		SAFETY MEETING		
	YES	NO	Subject:	

CONCERNS/ ACTIONS:

TEMPERATURE	
AM	**PM**

GROUND CONDITIONS (Wet, Dry, Frozen, Damp)

VISITORS (Name, Company, Reason)

SCHEDULE	
Completion Date	
Days Ahead	
Days Behind	

PROBLEMS/ DELAYS

SAFETY ISSUES

ACCIDENTS/ INCIDENTS (Who, Where, When, Contact)

SUMMARY OF WORK PERFORMED TODAY

SIGNATURE		TITLE	

EMPLOYEE	Craft	Contracted Hrs.	Overtime		Subcontractors	Craft	Hours Worked

EQUIPMENT ON SITE	No. Units	Working	
		Yes	No

MATERIALS DELIVERED	No. Units	Materials Rented	From & Rate

NOTES

DATE	/ /	**DAY**	M	T	W	T	F	S	Su

FOREMAN	

PROJECT/ JOB		CONTRACT No.	

WEATHER (Hot, Rain, Windy etc.)	**SAFETY MEETING**		

	YES	NO	Subject:

CONCERNS/ ACTIONS:

TEMPERATURE

AM	PM

GROUND CONDITIONS
(Wet, Dry, Frozen, Damp)

VISITORS (Name, Company, Reason)

SCHEDULE

PROBLEMS/ DELAYS

Completion Date	
Days Ahead	
Days Behind	

SAFETY ISSUES

ACCIDENTS/ INCIDENTS (Who, Where, When, Contact)

SUMMARY OF WORK PERFORMED TODAY

SIGNATURE		TITLE

EMPLOYEE	Craft	Contracted Hrs.	Overtime	Subcontractors	Craft	Hours Worked

EQUIPMENT ON SITE	No. Units	Working	
		Yes	No

MATERIALS DELIVERED	No. Units	Materials Rented	From & Rate

NOTES

SITE SAFETY CHECKLIST

DATE	/ /	DAY	M	T	W	T	F	S	Su

SITE

Safety Representative	
Emergency Phone Numbers Posted	
First Aid Supplies On Site	
Fire Extinguishers On Site	
Eye Wash Available	

SECURITY & PUBLIC SAFETY

Site Perimeter Fence	
Warning Signs Present	
Adequate Lighting	

CONTRACTORS

Designated Safety Officer	
Holding Regular Safety Meetings	
Familiar With Safety Procedures	
All Have Appropriate Permits	
All Contractors Are Familiar With Emergency Action Plan	

HOUSEKEEPING

Exits And Access Ways :Maintained / Unobstructed	
Toilet Facilities (Adequate Number)	
Storage Facilities For Tools	
Trash Piles	

FALL PROTECTION

Fall Protection Plans Available	
Positioning Devices	
Holes/ Openings Covered	
Are Guardrails Set Up Adequately	
Harnesses Are Worn Properly	

SCAFFOLDING

Competent Person Designated To Erect, Use, Dismantle	
Anchored Structure	
Proper Access (No Climbing Cross Bracing)	
Overhead Protection	
Guardrails	
All Pins In Place (Coupling Pins)	
Employees Trained	

ELECTRICALS

Power Tools In Good Working Condition	
Breakers Labeled, High Voltage Signs Posted And Adequate Access	
Installations Are Appropriate For Location (Weather, Flammable)	
Extension Cords With Grounding Conductor	
Location Of Power Lines Identified	
Exposed Live Parts Covered/Close	

SCAFFOLDING

Competent Person Designated (Erect, Use, Dismantle)	
Anchored Structure	
Proper Access (NO CLIMBING CROSS BRACING)	
Overhead Protection (Access Under Deck Barricaded, Extended Toe Boards, Mesh)	
Guardrails	
All Pins In Place (Coupling Pins)	
Employees Trained	

ADDITIONAL SITE SAFETY CHECKLIST

NOTES

NOTES

NOTES

NOTES

Made in the USA
Las Vegas, NV
23 November 2020